THE
UNIVERSITY
OF
TORONTO
A Souvenir

THE UNIVERSITY OF TORONTO

A Souvenir

Text by Ian Montagnes

Photographs by Rudi Christl

Toronto
Oxford University Press
1984

CREDITS The University of Toronto Archives: pages 2, 3, 4-5, 6, 7, 8, 9, 10-11, 12, 15, 16, 17, 19, 20, 21. The City of Toronto Archives (James Collection of Early Canadiana): pages 13,14. Professor S.B. McIver, Department of Zoology, University of Toronto, and Professor Frances W. Doane, editor, *Bulletin of the Microscopical Society of Canada*: page 75. The illuminated map on page 18 was photographed by courtesy of Hart House. The map on pages 22-3 was adapted from one published by the Department of Information Services, University of Toronto. All photo images by Rudi Christl were produced with the latest Pentax equipment. The University of Toronto crest on page v is reprinted by permission of the University of Toronto.

CANADIAN CATALOGUING IN PUBLICATION DATA

Montagnes, Ian

The University of Toronto : a souvenir

ISBN 0-19-540449-1

1. University of Toronto – Description – Views.
I. Christl, Rudi   II. Title.

LE3.T533M66   1984   378.713'541   C83-099293-6

©Oxford University Press (Canadian Branch) 1984
OXFORD is a trademark of Oxford University Press
1 2 3 4 – 7 6 5 4
Printed in Hong Kong by
SCANNER ART SERVICES INC. TORONTO

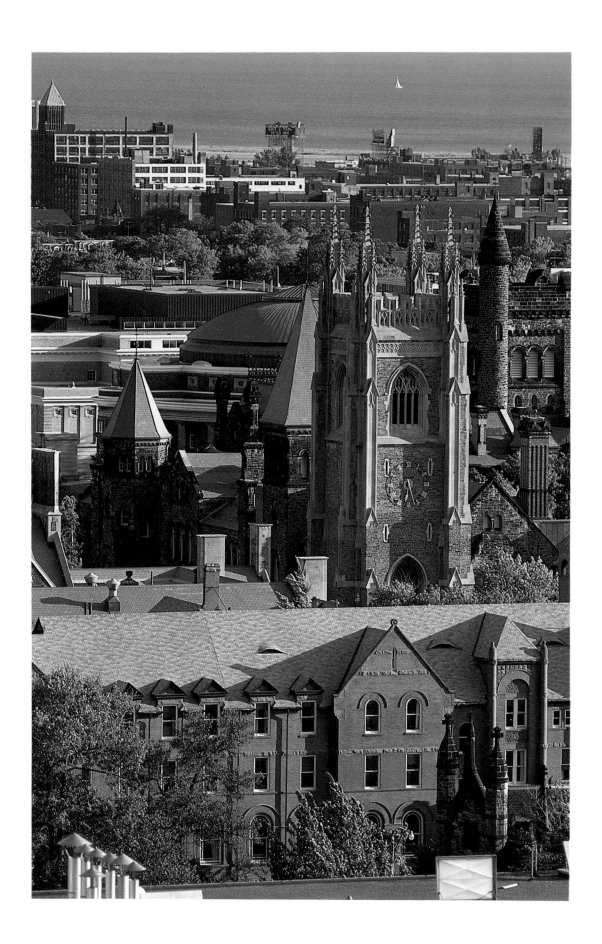

Introduction

Walking through the University of Toronto campus, I sometimes think what fun it might be to photograph parts of its buildings and show them to friends as souvenirs of an international tour—a rooftop of University College as a château on the Loire, a window of Hart House as a stately home in England, some of the tiles from the old library as a palazzo in Italy, the columns of Convocation Hall as a monument in Paris, and so on. The older buildings of the campus have an attractive diversity that makes such a fantasy possible, and although the newer ones too often lack charm, even they have their own distinctive characters. There has been no attempt to force the structures of the university into a single mould. In its physical appearance, as in other aspects of its life, the University of Toronto demonstrates its belief in freedom of expression. This diversity Rudi Christl has captured with an observant, imaginative eye.

There is another, more recent, diversity to be found in the lecture halls and labs. A couple of generations ago, Toronto drew its students mainly from the city and rural Ontario. Those undergraduates who could not return home for Christmas were a tiny minority who could fit easily into the Great Hall of Hart House for a special holiday dinner. Today, the majority of the students still come from Metropolitan Toronto and other parts of Ontario. But the rest have journeyed from all the provinces and many of the states of North America, from nearly one hundred countries on the other continents. The campus is a kaleidoscope of skin colours and, in summer, of costumes—a junior fellow of Massey College, black gown trailing behind him, bicycles past Nigerians in loose, colourful shirts; a visitor from India, in flowing pink sari, glides past a co-ed in jeans and a Banff T-shirt.

No other university—perhaps no other location—in Canada attracts so many people from so many places for so many different reasons. Some have come thousands of miles to learn about public health programs or the construction of concrete roadways, others have taken a streetcar ride to hear about the cultures of their ancestors in Portugal or the Ukraine, or to see for themselves the fossil record or the living cell. Depending on their chosen fields, students from far or near may be reading the cuneiform boasts of ancient Babylonian monarchs, the philosophies of ancient Greece, the epics of medieval France, the plays of Elizabethan England, the politics of Commonwealth statesmen, computer print-outs from an economic model, geological clues in rocks carried back from the moon, texts on Japanese management practice. They may be using the university's full-scale opera stage or its twenty-thousand-acre

The university grounds once stretched to Yonge Street. This gate to them stood at Yonge and College Streets in the 1870s.

forest, a six-hundred-ton materials tester, an electron microscope, a microfilm reader, an astronomical telescope, a laser, one of the eleven teaching hospitals.

Toronto is a big university—the biggest in this country, large by any standard. Its present size is the result of force-feeding, a political decision by government in the 1950s and '60s to meet the requirements of a growing economy and population. In one decade, the University of Toronto virtually doubled facilities built over the previous century, razing Victorian structures in mid-town and replacing them with high-rise labs, extending itself on two new campuses hugging wooded river valleys in the suburbs. Size has academic advantages:

in the depth and breadth of courses offered, the range of facilities, the quality of faculty. It has disadvantages, too. Students, and staff, can be lost in the system. But diversity tempers size at Toronto. Not that it results from any grand scheme. It just happened.

Certainly John Graves Simcoe, Lieutenant-Governor of Upper Canada and founder of the city of Toronto, could have had no such intention when he proposed in 1793 a university that might 'have great influence in civilizing the Indians and, what is more important, those who corrupt them'. Nor, even more certainly, did John Strachan, Bishop of Toronto, when he secured a royal charter for King's College—the immedi-

In those days Taddle Creek ran through the campus. Just east of University College it was dammed to form a pleasant pond.

The university in 1876, as painted by Lucius R. O'Brien. ▷

ate ancestor of the University of Toronto—in 1827 and gave it an uncompromisingly Anglican and Establishment cast. The reformers who thwarted Strachan's plans a generation later knew only that they wanted a provincial university free of church affiliation; and when they laid the cornerstone of the university building in an open field north of the city in 1856, it was largely to secure the endowment they had obtained for it in stone and mortar before it could be taken away. For another generation the building we know as University College was the entire university—a turreted Romanesque fantasy of a college set beside a clear-running stream, with a chemistry laboratory that looked

from the outside like a twelfth-century abbot's kitchen. The men who studied there—no women were admitted until 1884—were tough physically as well as mentally: the meals were skimpy, the residence rooms heated only by small coal fires, the distractions of the city a long walk away.

From that nucleus the University of Toronto grew gradually, more by aggregation than by plan. Beginning in the 1880s, it gathered within an academic federation three other universities that had been founded, about the same time as itself, in affiliation with churches—Victoria (Methodist), Trinity (Anglican), and St Michael's (Roman Catholic). They were strong

The university militia, Company K of the Queen's Own Rifles, just returned from service against Louis Riel in July 1885.

in the humanities but couldn't afford to expand in the rapidly growing sciences and the newer social sciences: federation allowed them to retain individuality and considerable autonomy, while acquiring for their students all the curricular variety of the provincial university. In the same period the university began teaching medicine and dentistry, both previously offered elsewhere in Toronto; it also absorbed the neighbouring School of Practical Science and renamed it the Faculty of Applied Science and Engineering (still sometimes known as School). Other professional training and faculties appeared in response to public need. Early in the twentieth century, Ontario was unlocking its natural wealth:

let there be, said the province, a Mining Building and a Faculty of Forestry. Was something more than hospital training needed for nurses in the 1930s? Well then, let us start a school of nursing. And so it continued—usually cautiously (it took more than half a century for Architecture to be weaned from Engineering and established as a faculty on its own), in response to changing interests in research (a small wind tunnel in the 1920s evolved into the Institute for Aerospace Studies, an active partner in the U.S. space program) or in response to changes in the community and the world (the last two decades have seen heightened interest in Italian language and literature as Toronto's population

The graduating class of 1883 in modern languages. Sir Daniel Wilson, president of the university, is in the centre.

diversified, in modern Asian history and the economics of developing nations as the global balance tipped). Over the years were added divisions that teach and study business management, child development, education, law, library and information science, music, pharmacy, physical and health education, and social work.

In its explosive growth during the 1960s, the university continued to find virtue in diversity. It rejected a planned battery of high-rise student residences and opened further colleges—New (so called because it was the first in three-quarters of a century) and Innis (named after a distinguished scholar) on campus, Scarborough and Erindale approximately twenty miles to the east and west (each of these semi-self-contained but drawing on the larger parent). The long-established Extension Division, through which thousands of Ontarians had earned their degrees in those most difficult of ways, by evening classes and correspondence courses, was reconstituted as Woodsworth College. To the larger body also was grafted Massey College, a home for graduate students of great promise—a gift from the Massey Foundation echoing its gift half a century earlier of Hart House, a centre mainly for undergraduates. And there sprang up a host of interdisciplinary centres and institutes—for medieval studies, for biomedical engin-

One February evening in 1890 fire swept through University College. This was the scene next morning. The college was rebuilt over the next year and a half.

eering, for drama, for criminology, for public-policy analysis, for a dozen other broad areas of human imagination and public interest.

Confusing? Of course it is. That's the whole point. There is no monolithic University of Toronto. It is a network of federation, confederation, affiliation, of baronies, satrapies, prefectures. It reflects its country. Canada is a cultural and political mosaic; the University of Toronto is an academic mosaic. Like Canada, it does not always work well—but then, some might argue that neither *should* work, just as the bumble-bee, according to aerodynamic theory, should not fly. But it does work. Despite the fact that few people would

even pretend to understand all its complexities. Despite the story that expansion of the central administrative computer was held up some years ago because the department of philosophy refused to move its offices to make room for machines. It is the diversity of constituents in the aggregate we call the University of Toronto that gives it strength and character.

Of course there is a central administration—a representative Governing Council, a president and panoply of vice-presidents, a small (by business or government standards) civil service. For the university is the equivalent of a small city with a population of some fifty-five thousand full-time and part-time students and staff and

A panoramic view of the university and city early in the century. In the foreground, the Library and the Medical Building.

Smirle Lawson hurdles the McGill defence in October 1909. ▷ Varsity won that game and ended the season by defeating Ottawa Roughriders to win the first Grey Cup.

an annual operating budget in excess of four hundred million dollars. It has two hundred and twenty-five buildings on its three principal campuses, the vast majority of them on the one hundred and twenty-seven acres around St George Street. It has its own post office, newspaper, fire marshal, police force, sports teams and athletic complex, restaurants, theatres, workshops, radio stations, bookstores, publishing house, printing plant, chapels, groundskeepers, locksmiths, clubs, and residences. Its library system, five million volumes strong—from the most recent of specialized scientific journals to some of the earliest of printed books—is by far Canada's largest intellectual reposi-

tory and one of North America's largest research collections. On the mid-town campus that is ringed by offices and apartment towers, playing-fields and walks and gardens—even a few remaining vintage elms— refresh lungs and spirits. The Scarborough and Erindale campuses have preserved large tracts of parklands and woods. It takes organization to make all this work.

But most of us who have studied at the University of Toronto have no more than an amorphous sense of the large institution. Our memories and loyalties are smaller, more local. A sunny autumn afternoon in Varsity Stadium, standing to sing 'The Blue and White' after the Blues have scored a touchdown. The rowdy fellow-

To my Se___
With S___

Varsity vs. McGill 1909

Good friend Elizabeth
warms [...] best Wishes

A class in the Household Science Building, opened in 1912.

ship of the Lady Godiva Memorial Band and the School Cannon. The zaniness of the student shows, the Meds' Daffydil, Dentanics, Micketies, the U.C. Follies, or the Vic Bob. The annual utterings of Father Episkopon at Trinity. The first publication of a poem or short story in one of the campus literary magazines. The late-night deadlines of *The Varsity*. A debate in Hart House against a visiting statesman, or a concert in the Great Hall. An unexpected success in the lab. A sudden insight in the library. And nearly always one or two great teachers, with luck, more: men and women who shared their knowledge with us and infused their lectures with their passion for the subject.

This is the underlying bond that ties together the sprawling, multi-faceted, often creaky, sometimes flagging, sometimes unhappy, more often inspiring institution of the University of Toronto—a passion for knowledge. It manifests itself at different levels: a freshman hearing for the first time morality discussed in the objective contexts of philosophy; a medical student learning the physiology that will help her save lives; a team of future engineers experimenting with that most peculiar amalgam of useful and useless knowledge, the design, construction, and racing of reinforced-concrete canoes; a graduate student exploring the nature of plants by feeding them radioactive isotopes; a retired

Styles of co-ed costume and accommodation, about 1908.

professor revelling in a new translation of Goethe; a professor of chemistry with a world-wide reputation bombarding gases with light to examine the behaviour of the building blocks of matter; another professor, not yet so well known, discovering a new twist in the spiral of DNA, the chemical that holds the genetic code of life. Heady stuff for those who become addicted. No wonder then that in the common-rooms and coffee shops and pubs around the campus, students talk of dates and music and sports, but also of Kant and quarks and computer programs; or that the Faculty Club has a table where the habitués seem to speak in mathematics.

Over the years, Toronto has not done badly in trans-lating passion into achievement. The most famous dis-covery on its campus is still that of insulin, which since 1921 has enabled over one hundred million diabetics to lead more or less normal lives. Add to this, in the field of medicine, the creation of a specially balanced diet to keep well babies healthy, marketed as Pablum; advances in total body cooling, a key to open-heart surgery; leadership in the study of arthritic and rheumatic diseases; the development by a doctor of the first G-suit, which protected World War II fighter pilots from blackouts and is the basis of today's space suits; the building of the first electric heart pace-maker; the invention of an artificial larynx and a portable pancreas. There are scores

War has been a recurrent theme in the university, as in its society: cadets gather in front of Convocation Hall about 1917, during the 'war to end all wars'.

On 5 June 1924 the university dedicated Soldiers' Tower, a ▷ memorial raised by the alumni to honour their wartime dead.

more of such accomplishments in medicine and in the other sciences, both pure and applied—breakthroughs far less easy than these to comprehend, but each with its own impact on our well-being or on our knowledge of ourselves and of our universe.

Toronto's intellectual explorers have charted the growth of Canada's cities and the decline of her glaciers. They have searched the skies for binary star clusters and built North America's first electron microscope to unlock the world of the infinitely tiny. Continually, too, they have been concerned for the world about them as well as with that of the mind—no ivory tower, this. Members of the university community have been

vigorous in campaigns for civil liberties and nuclear disarmament. They were fighting pollution long before most of us recognized it as a threat. In the 1950s they diagnosed the sickness of the Great Lakes; in the 1960s they mobilized for clean air and water under the umbrella of Pollution Probe. More than this: professors invented a plastic that 'rots' in sunlight, developed a paper-making process that reduces waste-product pollution; students, with staff encouragement, built a pair of test-model non-polluting cars of the future, designed a machine that licks up oil spills.

And books. Some years ago, at an international academic gathering in Toronto, an Australian visitor asked

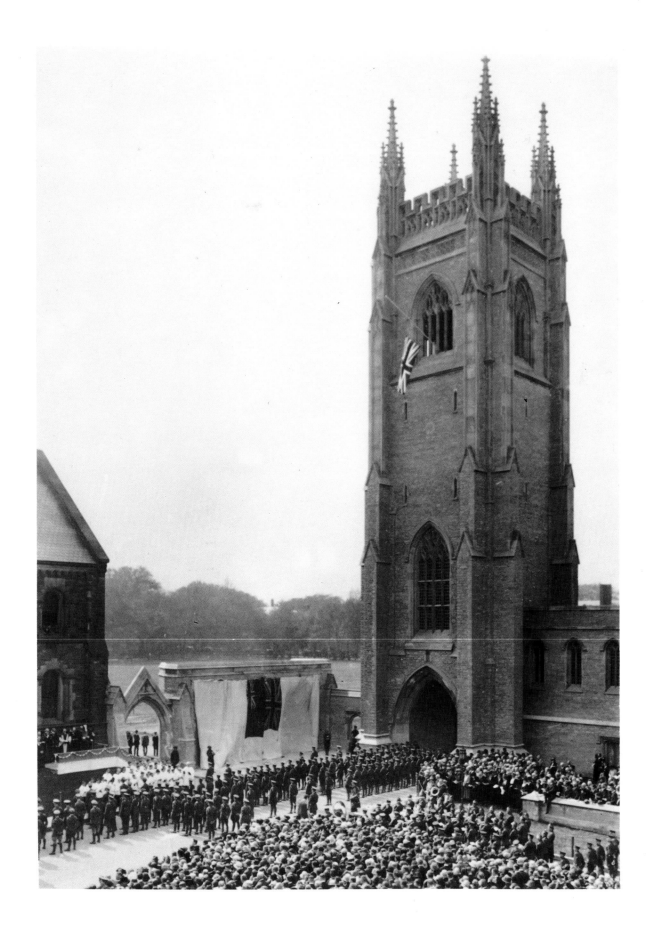

Charles H. Best and Sir Frederick Banting, with one of the first dogs in which they arrested diabetes by using insulin.

his host, 'Wasn't it a Toronto man who wrote *Christianity and Classical Culture*?' 'Yes. Charles Cochrane.' 'And didn't another Toronto man write *Puritanism and Liberty*?' 'A.S.P. Woodhouse.' 'Well,' said the Australian, 'any university that can produce two books like that in a generation should feel proud.' He might have added volumes by Harold Innis and Donald Creighton which gave a new perspective on Canadian history. Not to speak of Marshall McLuhan's *Gutenberg Galaxy* or the *Anatomy of Criticism* by Northrop Frye.

The university's accomplishments include its graduates. Among them are two Nobel laureates, three prime ministers, the first Canadian-born governor-general,

the first woman lieutenant-governor of Ontario, a clutch of provincial premiers and cabinet ministers at both levels of government, the present chief justice of Canada, and—to name only a few of the better known— novelists like Morley Callaghan and Timothy Findley, poets like Margaret Atwood and Dorothy Livesay, humorists like Stephen Leacock and Donald Harron, musicians like Glenn Gould and Teresa Stratas, painters like Lawren Harris and Ronald Bloore, actors like Kate Reid and Donald Sutherland. J.A.D. McCurdy was only eighteen months out of Engineering when, in 1909, at Baddeck, Nova Scotia, he became the first person to fly in the British Empire. Toronto's graduates have sur-

The original Engineering Building, the 'little red Schoolhouse',
about 1927. It was torn down in 1966.

veyed Canada's frontiers, built her railroads and bridges, created energy networks, pioneered broadcasting, designed aircraft. They are teachers, librarians, doctors, dentists, pharmacists, nurses, foresters, lawyers, social workers, psychologists, economists, diplomats, active citizens, concerned parents. There are one hundred and ninety thousand living alumni.

Enough of lists. Over more than a century of increasing activity, the University of Toronto has earned its epaulets in many and diverse ways. In the end what matters is its influence on individuals. It was said of a gifted educator that the ideal college would consist of him on one end of a log and a student on the other. In a sense, my memory of the University of Toronto is of sitting on one end of a number of logs, usually with someone interesting at the other end.

It is the place where I was first consistently treated as an adult. After a high school where everyone was addressed by last name only, I suddenly had a prefix—'Mr', the verbal equivalent of long trousers. I was accepted, and quickly given as much responsibility as I could handle, in the academic community and in a tight little knot of my peers. In both places I was encouraged to experiment—to try new ways and new ideas—and when, occasionally, this involved a brush with authority, the community came to the defence. I

<Alexander Scott Carter, who created the gold-splashed shields in the Great Hall, depicted the university of 1937 in an illuminated map that hangs in Hart House. This is a detail from it.

As director of Hart House Theatre, Robert Gill trained a generation for the Canadian stage. His first production, in 1947, was Shaw's Saint Joan. Charmion King played Joan. Others in the student cast were Donald Davis, David Gardner (with Miss King, ABOVE), Henry Kaplan, and William Hutt: all became prominent as actors or directors.

made friends I still have after thirty years. And I was exposed to people whose life revolved around the pursuit of knowledge. (Over the main doorway of Victoria College is carved 'The Truth shall make you free.' The University of Toronto recognizes more forms of truth than the old Methodists had in mind, but it pursues them with the same fervour.) People like Bertie Wilkinson, who shared in his lectures a lifetime of learning and love of the Middle Ages and had the charity, when after only two weeks on campus I presented an alternative theory for the decline and fall of the Roman Empire, to give that first essay an *alpha-minus*. R. MacGregor Dawson, striding into the large

lecture hall on Bloor Street in tweed jacket and black gown, recalling in stentorian tones (he couldn't speak quietly) the King-Byng constitutional battle from an insider's view. Nicholas Ignatieff, warden of Hart House, in a single sentence softly explaining the difference between private rights and public responsibilities. John Satterlee, grey-haired professor of physics, freezing daffodils and shooting off rockets in a madcap annual lecture on the wonders of liquid oxygen. Vincent Bladen, then midway through a record sixty years of teaching at the university, inflecting the 'dismal science' of economics with enthusiasm and wit: he did so until the day before he died in 1981.

◁ *Between numbers, at a formal dance sponsored by the Canadian Officers Training Corps in Hart House, late in the 1940s.*

The Blue and White Band, cheerleaders, pep rallies, and packed bleachers (not to speak of the odd hip-flask) supported the football Blues in the 1950s.

Today, styles have changed. 'Mr' and long trousers have both lost their significance. It is more difficult to make contact with some professors. But the community of scholarship, even if attenuated, still extends from first-year undergraduate to professor emeritus. Recently my son (who is at another Canadian university) was taken under the wing of one of his professors. I mentioned this to an acquaintance in the same field at the University of Toronto—a man who studies one-celled creatures that can eat oil spills and turn them into protein. He beamed. My son's new mentor had been his first graduate student at Toronto; and into that young man's education he had poured the gratitude he felt towards an older scientist (at yet a third,

American, university) who had given him his academic start. So the chain continues.

This last little story reminds us that although the University of Toronto may be singled out in a book, it does not stand alone. It is part of a national and international community and in that context it stands up pretty well. It is not as great as it sometimes pretends, but it is not as bad as its detractors sometimes claim. It preserves the old—buildings and knowledge—while exploring the new; it cultivates trees and flowers while growing in brick and mortar; it retains diversity and individuality; it nurtures first-rate minds. It is a good university, and those of us who have spent time in its halls have, for the most part, found it so.

St George Campus

Numerical directory and location guide

1 University College
2 Hart House/Soldiers' Tower
3 Sigmund Samuel Library
4 Medical Sciences Building
5 John P. Robarts Research Library
6 Convocation Hall
7 Faculty of Education
8 Cumberland House
9 Forestry Building
10 Architecture Building
11 Varsity Stadium
12 Varsity Arena
13 New College
14 Sidney Smith Hall
15 Massey College
16 Royal Conservatory of Music
17 Nursing Building
18 Woodsworth College
19 Flavelle House
20 Edward Johnson Building
   (Faculty of Music)
21 Athletic Complex
22 Galbraith Building
23 McLennan Physical Labs
24 Pharmacy Building
25 Innis College
26 St Michael's College
27 Victoria College
28 Emmanuel College
29 Knox College
30 Trinity College
31 St Hilda's College
32 Wycliffe College
33 Botany Building
34 Alumni House
35 Admissions Office

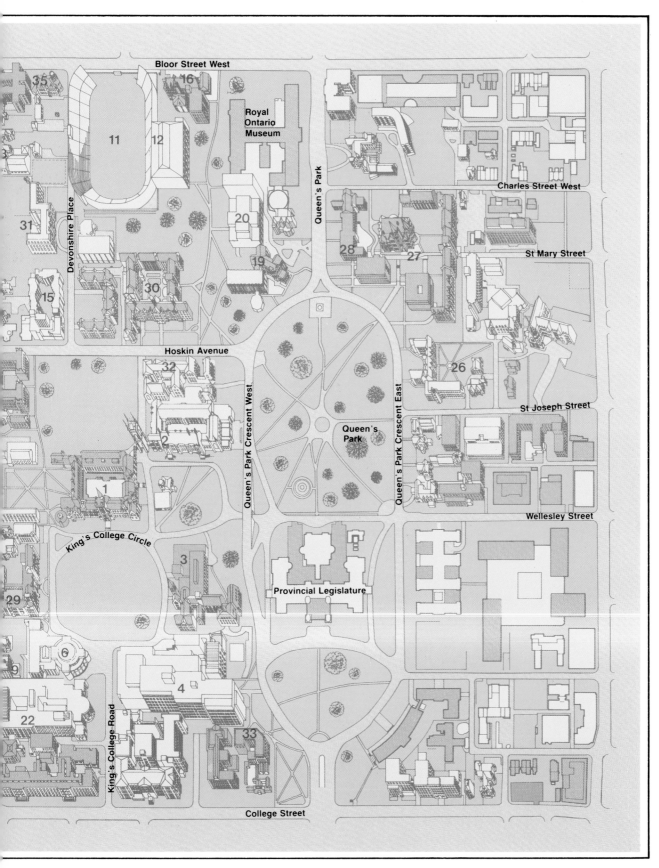

Bloor Street West

35

11   12

Royal Ontario Museum

Charles Street West

Devonshire Place

31

20

28   27

St Mary Street

15

19

30

St Joseph Street

Hoskin Avenue

32

26

Wellesley Street

Queen's Park

Queen's Park Crescent West

Queen's Park Crescent East

2

Queen's Park

1

King's College Circle

3

29

Provincial Legislature

9

6

22

King's College Road

4

33

College Street

A sunny beginning to university life: orientation at Victoria ▷
College.

University College, completed in 1859, was the first permanent home of the university and still stands at its heart.

Outside a men's residence: at Toronto, 'halls of ivy' is more than ▷ *a metaphor for the academic life.*

'The university is the glory of Toronto', the English novelist Anthony Trollope exclaimed after a visit in 1861. The university he saw consisted of only one building: what is now called University College. Its 'manly, noble structure' (Trollope again) contained all the lecture rooms, science labs, and offices; it had a residence wing and a convocation hall; it even had, it is said, a ghost, the spirit of a stonemason murdered by a rival in love during construction of the college in the 1850s. Around it stretched green parkland; a quarter of a century passed before another academic building rose nearby. All this is hard to remember on today's busy campus. But the college is still in heavy use and a delight to the eye. It is also one of the few buildings in the Toronto area to be designated a National Historic Monument.

◁ *In its exuberance the architecture of Victoria College echoes the institution's name.*

The twin red towers are sheltered by Victoria's newer buildings from city traffic.

Victoria is one of three smaller universities that federated with the University of Toronto late in the last century. Its first fifty years were spent in Cobourg, some sixty-five miles east of its present site (students still sing of life 'on the old Ontario strand'); and there, in 1841, it conferred the first university degree earned in Upper Canada. But by the 1880s the costs of teaching experimental science had outstripped the means of a private Methodist college. Reluctantly, agreement was reached to federate and move to Toronto. Continuing individuality was proclaimed in the new structure, splendidly high-Victorian in design. Since then, libraries, residences, and teaching halls have sprung up around the main building. In this campus within a campus, Victoria has maintained a vigorous pursuit of the humanities—nurturing, among others, Canada's most celebrated literary scholar, Northrop Frye.

Hart House at night. ▷

Flavelle House. The modern wing is a library.

An alcove in Hart House: Tudor architecture to be lived in. ▷

Several university buildings were once private homes —sturdy, well-proportioned reminders of a time when the streets within the campus were among the city's finest residential avenues. None is grander than the Beaux Arts mansion built at the turn of the century by Joseph Flavelle, a millionaire meat-packer who later won a baronetcy for supervising the production of munitions during World War I. Torontonians, unimpressed, and recalling the source of Flavelle's money, called it 'Porker's Palace'. Now it is occupied by the Faculty of Law.

Hart House was never a private residence, but it was designed on the model of Tudor domestic architecture, as a place to be lived in—that is why it was called a house. (The first word in its name recalls Hart Massey, builder of agricultural equipment, whose bequest made the building possible.)

◁ *The Great Hall of Hart House.*

Hart House quadrangle.

There is nothing quite like Hart House at any other university in the world. It has been studied ever since it opened in 1919, often emulated, but never equalled. Around one quadrangle it nurtures the body, spirit, and mind. It has dining-rooms, gymnasia, a swimming pool. It has its own small chapel. It has a fine collection of Canadian paintings, built up over the years to hang in its common-rooms. Its Sunday concerts attract musicians of world class. Its debates are attended by prime ministers. It offers rooms for browsing in books and magazines or for listening to records. It sponsors clubs for archery and amateur radio, photography and scuba diving, bridge and chess, and more. Most remarkably, it has always been run by committees of students, faculty members, and alumni in a common fellowship— with the students in the majority. The building, fully equipped, was a gift to the university from the Massey Foundation. It was so unusual that, shortly after it opened, Charles Best was invited to speak at Harvard on two topics: one was his recent discovery, with Frederick Banting, of insulin; the other was the institution of Hart House.

◁ *Fitness class in a Hart House gym.*

Soccer on the front campus.

Football is the traditional college sport, and so it was for most of this university's history. When the Blues played in Varsity Stadium a generation ago, they filled the stands and their victories made banner headlines in the evening newspapers. But styles change. The rah-rah spirit has weakened; interests have broadened. Toronto competes in more than twenty intercollegiate sports, and generally does well. After field hockey was introduced as a women's sport in 1960, the team played twenty consecutive seasons without a loss. The men's swimming team has an even more enviable record—twenty-three successive provincial championships as this was written. The hockey Blues are also consistent winners. More than one hundred and fifty students or graduates have represented their country in the Olympics, and three—runners Bruce Kidd and Bill Crothers, and marathon swimmer Cindy Nicholas—were chosen Canadian athletes of the year while still undergraduates. Beyond all this striving and achievement, there has come a new emphasis on non-competitive athletics. Fitness classes take over the gyms from basketball players; and from early morning to late evening the joggers are at it, outdoors when weather permits, indoors when it doesn't.

The arms of the University of Toronto and University College, carved and painted in 1891, in West Hall, U.C.

At the heart of the campus, Soldiers' Tower remembers the alumni ▷ dead of two world wars.

The past is never very far away on the St George campus. The older buildings incorporate history in their fabric. The newer ones, for the most part, bear the names of men and women—teachers, researchers, administrators, benefactors—who lent their talents to develop the university of today.

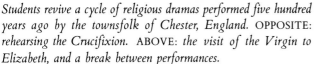

Students revive a cycle of religious dramas performed five hundred years ago by the townsfolk of Chester, England. OPPOSITE: *rehearsing the Crucifixion.* ABOVE: *the visit of the Virgin to Elizabeth, and a break between performances.*

Five hundred years ago, scenes like these would have been familiar. They come from the religious drama of the Middle Ages, the beginnings of English theatre. On campus, they represent painstaking scholarship channelled into enjoyable performance. They are the product of one of the most remarkable of the university's theatrical groups, Poculi Ludisque Societas (the Fellowship of Cup and Play), a gathering of staff and students of medieval literature and history, drama, and music.

The troupe is a living laboratory of early theatre, and as such has toured North America and Europe. In May 1983, in one of its most ambitious productions, it recreated the fifteenth-century Chester Cycle—twenty-six short plays depicting the story of the Bible. As in medieval England, the plays were set on wagons that moved in procession. Some of the players travelled hundreds of miles to take part in the Cycle. Some scholars crossed the Atlantic just to be part of the audience.

◁ *Within the college grounds stands an abstract 'Michael', by Anne Allardyce.*

Buildings of St Michael's College, Teefy and Carr Halls, viewed from Queen's Park Crescent.

St Michael's College runs eastward from the wrought-iron fence along Queen's Park Crescent over to Bay Street, sloping gently up to Clover Hill, the site of its beginnings and of St Basil's Church. Many of the older buildings reflect the French origins of the Basilian Fathers, who direct the college. Modern architecture is also well represented—even extremely modern sculpture. The heart of this eclectic campus, however, is Elmsley Place, a short avenue of Victorian houses, once the homes of prominent Canadians, now academic residences. St

Michael's was founded in 1852 as a Catholic community for the young men of Upper Canada. It has expanded to include two residential colleges for women, Loretto and St Joseph's, and to embrace the internationally famed Pontifical Institute of Mediaeval Studies. St Michael's continues to emphasize spiritual as well as intellectual development in its students. But it does not look only to the past or to St Thomas Aquinas. One of its best-known professors was that guru of the electronic age, Marshall McLuhan.

Sir Daniel Wilson men's residence.

The judges' stand at a Homecoming float parade.

Former members of the Blue and White Band have become a fixture of alumni celebrations.

The undergraduates enjoy Homecoming too: high spirits are ▷ evident in the annual float parade.

The university claims nearly two hundred thousand living graduates, and considers them all part of the family. In the fall it stages a Homecoming Party. There's usually a student-run float parade in the morning, a football game in the afternoon, and meals and parties before and after. Reunions involve classmates of fifty, sixty, even seventy years ago. Sometimes old-timers from the Blue and White Band get together to make music. But alumni do more than put on straw hats and blow horns. They gave the university Convocation Hall and Soldiers' Tower; more recently they have joined with government and business in funding new buildings and renovating old ones. They support scholarships and student loans, lectures and plays. They honour outstanding students and teachers. They volunteer time—indexing archives, teaching English to foreign students, counselling undergraduates, conducting campus tours. They sit on the Governing Council and other committees. They offer advice and encouragement. They link the university and its community.

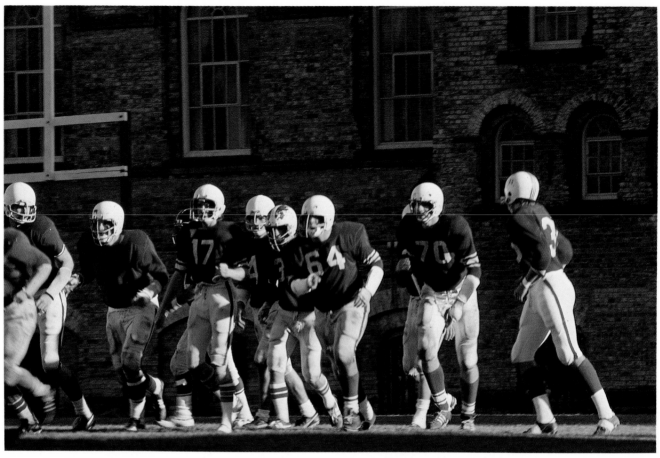

In the fall, colleges and faculties field their own football teams in competition for the Mulock Cup.

On a sprawling campus, a good deal of time between lectures may ▷ be spent walking.

Of all seasons on the campus, autumn is most joyful. The buildings and open spaces fill with new vigour after the summer quiet. Old friendships renew, and new ones come into being. Discoveries and challenges arise with new courses and new professors. The football team trains and practises, unburdened yet by injuries or defeats. There is a ferment of talk, dances, celebrations, sport. As weeks pass, the horse-chestnuts and acorns ripen and fall, and the black squirrels who treat the university as a giant preserve grow fat. Before too long, passage between buildings will be a matter for overcoats and snowboots; and after winter comes the bittersweet university spring, a mixture of warm evenings and late essays, embraces and examinations. But for the time being, the students walk relaxedly through grounds that glow in the autumn sun.

◁ *The Robarts Library: the smaller building on the right holds the rare book collection and university archives.*

Colour-coded stack shelves in the Robarts Library help researchers find their way around the collection.

Fifty libraries are scattered around the campus, some with buildings of their own, others containing highly specialized collections in a few rooms. They hold a bewildering array of reading: books and journals, maps, manuscripts, and microfiches, pages from the birth of printing, reports from the frontiers of science. There are more than five million items in the university-wide system. It is Canada's richest literary storehouse by far, and one of the largest on the continent. At its core stands the John P. Robarts Research Library, opened in 1973, devoted principally to research materials in the humanities and social sciences. Students call it Fort Book—a reference to its formidable fourteen storeys as well as to the care with which its collection is protected. It is one of their most valuable resources. The strength of a university depends as much on its library as on its people.

For everything from musicals to protest marches, notices in the lobby of Sidney Smith Hall seek student attention.

Throngs of students pass through the lobby of Sidney Smith Hall each day: it provides a natural focus for their many interests. The campus has scores of organizations—film and theatrical clubs, political and religious associations, folk-dance and national societies, plus a full spectrum of groups supporting public causes. Among them: an Alliance of Non-Zionist Jews, Amnesty International, the Canadian Anti-Soviet Action Committee, the Marxist Institute and the Trotskyist League, the Committee Against Racism, Justice for Children, the Lesbian and Gay Academic Society, a Meditation Society and an Outing Club, a Model United Nations, the Polish Workers Solidarity Committee, the U.C. Players' Guild, Science for Peace, the Vegetarian Cooking Club, and the Society for Creative Anachronism. The last-named preserves the art of knightly jousting.

Mens sana in corpore sano—a healthy mind in a healthy
body. An institution dedicated to the exercising of minds
also pays attention to physical development. The university's principal athletic complex fills a city block; there
are ancillaries in the colleges, in Hart House, at Erindale
and Scarborough. The campus has clubs and courses in
dancing, swimming, badminton, tennis, squash, boxing,
curling, golf, white-water canoeing, judo, and karate,
to begin with. It has co-educational programs in some
less traditional games, including touch football, broom-
ball, indoor soccer, and inner-tube water polo. It also
co-ordinates league competition at several levels in more
than thirty men's and women's sports between colleges,
faculties, and residences. This is one of the finest intra-
mural athletic programs in North America. Each year,
nearly ten thousand young men and women take advan-
tage of it to keep fit between bouts with the books.

◁ *For second-year students of architecture, the design of a pleasurable room is an engrossing problem.*

In the Faculty of Music, a Haydn quartet may be played for credit as well as enjoyment.

In a two-week period chosen at random, the university offered ten concerts, four exhibitions of art, a pair of one-act plays, a dozen film screenings, a poetry reading, a number of special lectures, an exhibition of architectural design, and a book sale, not to speak of a festival of the gentle martial arts. Many of these events were open to the public—one of the several ways in which the University of Toronto serves the wider community.

On the stage of the MacMillan Theatre, students of the Opera ▷ Division rehearse Arthur Benjamin's Prima Donna *under the direction of Michael Albano.*

The university feeds a population the size of a small city. A few
dining-rooms, like Trinity's Strachan Hall, are Gothic.

*Others are utilitarian, among them the cafeteria added in 1983 to
Sidney Smith Hall. All serve wholesome, if not gourmet, food.*

A view from the University College cloisters, once a men's residence. Across the quadrangle is the modern Laidlaw Wing.

The east staircase is a fine example of U.C.'s woodwork. Genera-▷ tions of student hands have polished the dragon at its foot.

On the evening of 14 February 1890, a servant in University College stumbled and dropped a lighted oil lamp. It shattered. Fire spread, quickly out of control, and by morning half the building was gutted. Reconstruction began at once; a year and a half later the college re-opened. More than the roof and timbers had been replaced. The interior was restored with loving detail. Woodcarvers had panelled its halls and festooned them in medieval style with a myriad of eccentric faces, weird animals, and abstract patterns. Their work can be enjoyed in fresh brilliance today, thanks to a major renovation during the 1970s.

The Science and Medicine Library and Sigmund Samuel Library: until 1973, these wings formed the main library of the campus.

Cumberland House, home of the International Student Centre,▷ was restored as a project of the Rotary Clubs of Toronto.

Students come to the University of Toronto from nearly a hundred countries. They may find its language difficult, its customs strange, its snow and ice a shock. The International Student Centre exists to help them. It offers advice before and after they arrive, provides a place for their meetings and discussions, and runs its own program of activities. Its home is very Canadian: Frederic W. Cumberland, the architect of University College, built it for himself in 1860 and lived in it for twenty-one years. Judging by the reception rooms, he did so in some style. Today the rooms may be used for lists of housing, meetings of the Turkish Student Association or the Korean Intervarsity Christian Fellowship, a Chinese folk-song group, a course in English as a second language, a ping-pong tournament, a poetry reading, a film about Canada, or a planning session for a campus international soccer league. In the kitchen, someone may be cooking a Greek dinner.

In winter, cross-country skiers take over the back campus jogging track. ▷

Within an institution officially non-denominational ('godless', its early critics called it), religion flourishes. Five theological colleges federated or affiliated with the University of Toronto, and co-operating in the Toronto School of Theology, prepare candidates for ordination: Emmanuel (United Church), Knox (Presbyterian), St Michael's (Roman Catholic), Trinity and Wycliffe (both Anglican). All have handsome chapels (one outstanding example appears on page 71), as do Hart House and Massey College. Many a graduate has returned to be married in one of them. The Jewish Students' Union and the Roman Catholic Newman Centre have their own buildings and programs. The Student Christian Movement, for over half a century, has combined religion with strong social awareness. Within this traditional Ontario matrix are found other world faiths: Eastern Orthodox Christians, Baha'is, Buddhists, Hindus, and Muslims worship on the campus.

Vaulting of Soldiers' Tower.

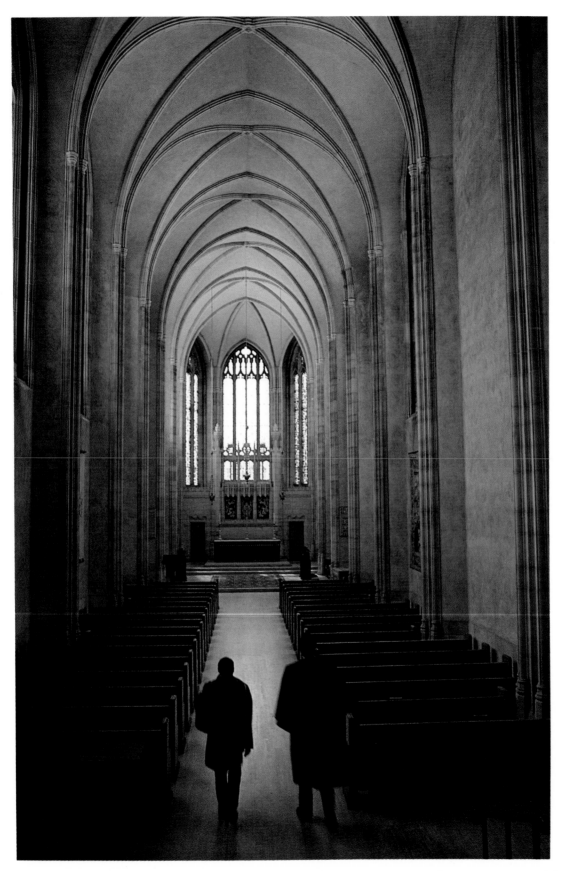

Trinity College Chapel.

The Newman Centre stands at a campus crossroads. ▷

◁ *Laser pulses lasting a trillionth of a second probe the fleeting motion of atoms and molecules.*

An electron microscope captures the fine details of the head of a female mosquito, chief carrier of malaria in India.

A casual visitor to the campus doesn't see the research that is constantly under way, any more than the visitor to an electrical generating station can see the turning of its giant turbines. Yet the academic staff is busy. They are probing the universe, from the heavens to the insides of atoms. They are studying the nature of humanity, from early history to the present. They are helping us to learn more about ourselves and our country. They are making discoveries that will save lives, improve world health, preserve the environment, contribute to material well-being. Only rarely do the results make the newspapers. Yet behind office and laboratory doors, and in libraries and at field sites scattered around the world, the work goes on, exemplifying (as a recent national publicity campaign put it) that 'Canada's energy is mindpower'.

Reinforced concrete stands in elegant repose before the Medical Sciences Building.

Reinforced concrete is tortured to the breaking point in this engi- ▷ *neering test machine.*

About a third of the students at the University of Toronto are enrolled in its professional faculties—training-grounds for engineers, architects, and foresters; doctors, dentists, nurses, and pharmacists; lawyers, musicians, teachers, business managers, librarians, and social workers. Competition for a place in these faculties is keen. But their reputations rest on more than teaching: they are also centres for advanced study in their various fields. The giant tester on the opposite page, for example, is used both for instruction and for experimentation leading to improved structural design. It belongs to the Department of Civil Engineering. This department was involved in one of the most visible of all the products of the university's multi-faceted research—the world's largest free-standing structure, Toronto's CN Tower.

◁ *Nine thousand tons of concrete, pre-cast and placed at random, form the patterned walls of the Medical Sciences Building.*

The School Cannon makes one of its infrequent appearances, chained to burly honour guards as a precaution against theft.

Legends linger of friendly, but sometimes violent, rivalry between professional faculties, especially between medical and engineering students. There are tales of mammoth free-for-alls, of stolen trophies and of hostages taken, of raiding parties armed with snowballs or firehoses. That was in the past. Today's campus is more staid, more geared to purposeful study and high marks. But the engineers, who also work hard, retain a spirit of zany rowdiness. Its symbolic focus is the School Cannon, diminutive but noisy, which is fired on ceremonial occasions. Invariably it is accompanied by the Lady Godiva Memorial Band, motley and also noisy, which may perform on almost any occasion.

A quiet corner of University College: the dean's residence and ▷
Howard Ferguson Hall.

Academics of the past guard a Trinity doorway.

At Trinity, gowns are de rigueur—*even over blue jeans.* ▷

Trinity College was founded in 1851 by the Anglican Establishment of Upper Canada, and still retains something of a High Church, aristocratic cast. It is a college of traditions—some peculiar to itself, others, like the wearing of black academic gowns, reminders of another century. Its handsome main building is doubly a reference to the past, for it is not only Gothic: it is a 1920s reincarnation of the original college building that stood a couple of miles to the southwest on Queen Street. Still, Trinity has no difficulty in poking fun at its own pretentions ('We are the salt of the earth', its irreverent cheer begins) and its small, tightly knit community attracts some of the university's best students. These days by no means all of them are either Establishment or Anglican.

◁ Free-form walls enclose the quadrangle of New College.

The University Bookroom offers more than books.

During the 1960s the university doubled in size. It needed places for the additional students to live; and for a time there was talk of a phalanx of high-rise residences, planned like apartment blocks and just as faceless. The idea made sense financially, but not academically. Instead, the university added colleges: residences, to be sure, but with their own social and intellectual identities. The first of these, opened in 1965, was called New College. The name, while seemingly uninspired, stretched back centuries in precedent. The first New College was founded at Oxford in 1379. It is still going strong.

Externals of research: elegant doorway of the Botany Department greenhouse; (OPPOSITE) thrusting modernity of the Physics complex.

*The terrace in front of Trinity College announces the ▷
arrival of spring. The towers recall an older Trinity.*

The verdant campus of Erindale College is just thirty minutes by car from downtown Toronto.

At Erindale, banners attest to the variety and centrality of the ▷ curriculum.

At Erindale College, meadow grass stands shoulder-high and the Credit River flows beneath wooded slopes. Within the limits of the campus, staff and students have identified one hundred and thirty-eight kinds of birds, three hundred and seventy-five different trees and plants, sixty species of ants. The two hundred and forty acres in Mississauga are a resource for biologists and a recreational haven for students. Erindale also has its own library, science and language labs, computer, electron microscopes, lecture halls, theatre, bookstore, and art gallery. It is virtually a small university in its own right, linked to its parent by close ties and hourly buses. It is a reminder, in a sense, of a time when the huge midtown campus was itself a green parkland. But only in a sense. At Erindale, the structure marked with a crescent moon is a million-dollar laboratory. It was built specially to study lunar rocks and dust brought back to Earth by the Apollo astronauts.

Scarborough College rises high over its three-hundred-acre campus in the east of Metropolitan Toronto.

A styrofoam model of muscle fibre in a lobster's leg helps Scarborough students understand differentiation in cells. ▷

Scarborough College opened in the fall of 1966 with an international reputation already achieved. Its building was one of the most famous of the decade, the subject of national and international architectural discussion. Not everyone liked it: the stark concrete design warred with almost every traditional concept of what a college should be. But in the interplay of natural light and rough walls, of large meeting places and enclosed pedestrian streets, of grand vistas over the Highland Creek ravine, John Andrews gave the new college excitement and adventure. Ironically, the physical construction diminished the impact of the underlying educational experiment. Canada had never before had a college established in the same metropolitan community as its parent but separated by roughly twenty miles. Scarborough and Erindale (which opened the following year) were endowed with the strengths and reputation of the University of Toronto; but they remained close to the suburbs of which they are a part, and there they have developed their own programs and identities.

◁ *Innis College may lack a quadrangle, but it does have an open college green.*

Philosopher's Walk links busy Bloor Street with the centre of the campus.

Harold Innis, who died in 1952, was arguably the greatest scholar Canada has produced—a man of strong nationalism and social conscience, with a mind that swept from the cod fisheries and fur trade of early Canada to the media of communication and spread of empires in the ancient world. The college named after him in 1964 has shown the same readiness to test new ideas. It developed the first writing lab in the university, the first creative-writing course, the first co-op student residence; it was first to give students parity on a college council.

This character is reflected in its building. At one end it is modern, the kind of architecture that leaves air ducts exposed. But push on, past the informal auditorium, through skylit gallerias, and you find yourself in Victorian housing that might have been torn down but instead has been fused into the structure, binding it into its streetscape. Innis students are apt to be as unconventional as their college. Their enjoyment of it echoes in the newspaper they publish sporadically. They call it the *Innis Herald.*

Freedom of speech is an essential quality of any university, whether the cause be the evangelical Anglicanism of a Wycliffe College (LEFT) or an international peace movement. The principle has only rarely been threatened at the University of Toronto. Then it has been stoutly defended.

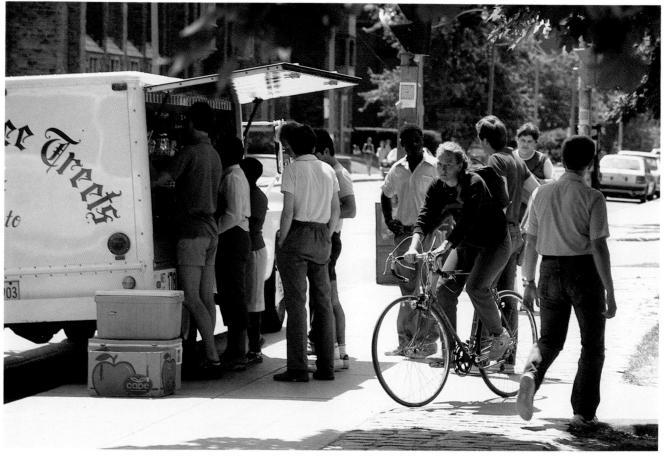

Lunch-wagons on St George Street.

The Koffler Student Services Centre. ▷

A large student body requires a substantial system of support. Some needs are simple—perhaps nothing more than a snack that can be supplied by curbside private enterprise. Others involve full-time professional staffs— to help students find housing off campus that is reasonably priced and free from discrimination; to stock the textbooks for thousands of specialized courses; to care for illnesses and injuries; to offer counselling at times of emotional stress; to ensure that the disabled can make their way into university buildings; to help students choose a career and find a job. In 1984, conversion began of the former Metro Toronto Reference Library into the Koffler Student Services Centre, a home for many of these services and a focus for student life in the southwest corner of the campus.

Eventually there comes the last spring as an undergraduate: the last essay, the last lecture, the last quiet talk in a corner of the campus, the last examination. With luck graduation follows: the black gown; the procession (if it is a nice day, and usually it is) across the front campus and into Convocation Hall; the formal academic entry of the faculty in multi-coloured caps and gowns from a host of universities; the Latin phrases of a centuries-old ritual; the moment of kneeling before the chancellor. The hood descends quickly. Then back to a seat on the rise. It's all over. Except, of course, for ...

... the pride and pleasure of friends and relatives;

... the lessons learned, not all in the classroom;

... the memories.